Know Yourself and learn to think

2 books in 1

1. manage your thoughts

2. Know Yourself

Ray Crystal

Know Yourself

**manage your thoughts,
uses analytical thinking and creative
thinking**

Ray Crystal

Know Yourself through

Thought patterns

Remove Negative Influences Cut Off Destroying Thoughts

Negative energy is everywhere. You can find it at every turn. Negative energy can take the form of unhappy people, violent content on television, or even environmental damage. You can see this consistently. No matter where you go, you will encounter charges of negative energy.

And while there isn't much, you can do to stop negative energy from swirling around in the world, and there is plenty that you can do to stop it from taking over your mind. When you find yourself immersed in a hostile environment, it is straightforward to get caught up in the situation's negativity.

For instance, you are working in a very hostile environment. Your boss and co-workers aren't getting along, which leads to an overall unpleasant atmosphere. At this point, you have one of two choices, you either let that get to you, or you don't. Of course, it's not quite that simple.

One of the most effective ways to avoid being brought down by this type of atmosphere is to stop it from getting to you merely. You can learn to recognize the onset of negative thoughts and emotions. When you do, you can nip them in the bud. You can make use of mantras such as "negative energies can't touch me" or "negative thoughts are like a ship passing in the night."

In other words, don't let negative thoughts pull up a chair and have a seat. If you allow them to do that, you are opening the door to trouble. The main thing to keep in mind is that you are the master of your thoughts and emotions. The only way something can get to you is if you let it.

However, indeed, a highly hostile environment will undoubtedly charge you with negative energy. In that case, it is always a great idea to have ways in which you can unload those energies. That is why pleasant activities are needed at the end of the day. That way, you can simply let go of the energies which are negatively affecting you.

Secrets to

Successfully Tame

Your Thoughts

If people knew that succeeding in life depended on their actions, they would be less likely to worry about their lives. At times, we go through life with regrets and anxiety. We don't feel ready to let go of the feelings that we have embedded within us. Concerning our future, we worry about tomorrow, but a large number of people don't know the power that they have. The power that you have within you can quickly become a destructive force or a constructive force that will push you to succeed in life. You have the power to control your life and live it as you wish. What you think about is what you become. If you keep thinking that you will always struggle in life, rest assured that you will struggle to keep things afloat. Conversely, if you genuinely believe that everything will fall into place and that your time will come for you to enjoy life, expect to live a life full of optimism.

Listen to Yourself

To tame your thoughts, start by listening to yourself. Do this as though you were explaining something to other people. How would you want to tell other people about the story of your life? Without a doubt, you would want to talk about everything that you have done well. No one would want to tell others negative stories about themselves. Therefore, you should adopt a similar attitude when listening to yourself. Focus on treating yourself with the same respect that you would expect from other people. This means that you should strive to focus on thoughts that put you in a positive light.

Your Inner Self is Listening

Besides, you should always bear in mind that your inner self is listening to your thoughts; this is the inner you. So, if you continue thinking about negative things, your inner self will listen and conform to how you expect it to behave. When thinking positively, it will also listen to you and adapt to help you perceive life with optimism. Therefore, before blaming other people for the bad things that are happening to you, remember that there is someone within you who is listening to your self-talk.

Befriend Your Emotional Guidance System

The point here is that you should pause every time you notice that your emotions have changed. You should take some time to evaluate your emotions and the next thoughts before they gain momentum. The effect of this is that it will help you develop an attitude of thinking twice before doing anything.

Before doing anything, you will reflect
on whether what you're about to do is
favorable or not. You increase the
likelihood of making the right decisions
without allowing emotions to cloud your
judgment.

Find Your Stop Signs

Another practical tip that can make a
difference in how you think is
visualizing stop signs that signal to you
that you should stop thinking about
something. Your stop signs will warrant
that you regain your senses and avoid

thinking about your past or worrying about your future. The best way of using these stop signs is to remind you that your thoughts are not helping to build you up. For instance, you can come up with a stop sign that reminds you that you are overthinking about events that prevent you from being happy. It might take some time for you to master how to use these stop signs, but the outcome will be rewarding as it will enhance your self-awareness.

Consider Words as Your Nutrition

When thinking about improving our health, we know perfectly that eating right can only be done. The foods that you choose to eat have an impact on your health. In the same manner, the words that float around in your mind impact your mental health. This means that it is essential that you control the information that you feed into your mind. For example, watching horrific content on television might not be as entertaining as you think. In the long run, this will harm how you think and the thoughts that frequent your mind.

Remind Yourself with Affirmations

Becoming the master of your mind also demands that you stay on top of your game. You have to keep yourself engaged in festive gear. Sure, there are instances when you might slip up and think negatively, but with the right affirmations, you will feel unstoppable. Have these affirmations in areas where you can easily see them. Pin them next to your files in your office. Before going to bed, remind yourself of your higher purpose by reading out these affirmations to yourself. They can eliminate anxiety and soothe you to sleep better.

Take Out the Trash

Increasing your self-awareness about your thoughts will give you the advantage of identifying unnecessary thoughts and emotions. When you do this steadily, you will find it easier to declutter your mind. The notion of taking out the trash shouldn't drive you to overthink about your past. Instead, the point here is to develop an attitude where you simply admit that some thoughts are

not worth holding on to. Practice
meditation exercises as a method of
increasing your self-awareness. This is
the best way of raising your antennas
high enough to pick any signals of
unwanted thoughts in your mind.

Pursue Meaning Over Pleasure

There is a good reason why you should
strive to be happy. Most people have
never realized that there are adverse
effects of focusing too much on striving
for positivity. Sure, we all want our lives
to be full of happiness. However, we

should come to terms with the fact that too much of anything is detrimental. This also applies to happiness. When we go about chasing happiness, we surround ourselves with all the things that can keep us entertained and full of joy. The downside of this kind of life is that it can blind us to unrealistic optimism.

Flex Your Muscle Memory

Technology has changed the way we access information in today's world. The digital devices that we have been introduced to make it easy for us to

consume information than ever before.
However, this affects our muscle
memory since we rely too much on these
devices. You can find Millennials
struggling with simple calculations
where they have to turn to their
smartphones. According to a study, to
some extent, seniors from the Baby
Boomer generation have better memory
compared to Millennials.

Take Control Over Your Thought Patterns

A "controlled thinking" mindset helps you to shift your focus intentionally. It allows you to determine your performance, rather than getting stuck replaying negative experiences in your head. You have to purposefully choose to focus on what you want instead.

In order to choose where you want to put your attention, you need to take control of your mind, thoughts, and emotions. You are only as stuck or as free as your mindset allows you to be. It is the story of good or bad experiences your mind tells you. It is the story of your life. It is the imprint of your mind.

The mind is an incredible machine. When given the right kind of input, it can produce amazing results. It is a habitual learner. It wants to adapt to its environment, including whatever patterns of thoughts, emotions, and actions you expose it to. It can also adapt to change. As its owner, you have the power to rewrite the story. You can choose to override the negative, limiting thoughts and emotions. You can decide to tell a different story and one that will empower you. You must intentionally choose to change your thinking and take control of your life.

To shift your mindset, you must first identify your habitual thoughts and emotions and then learn to shift them intentionally (not simply by willpower) by creating a better story.

You take control of where you focus
your attention. You can choose to think
or you can choose to feel. When you
choose to think and feel the right things,
you take control of your story, you write
a different ending, and you define your
life.

The key to transformation lies in you. It
all starts with the story your mind tells
you. Your mind is defined by your
thoughts and emotions. You are a
habitual thinker. You do not typically
think of something once and decide to
never think about it again. Your thoughts

initiative your emotions which in turn shape your responses and behaviors. Because your mind is a "habitual" learner, it will automatically and repetitively go to the place where you decide to take it.

You take control of where you focus your attention. You can choose to think or you can choose to feel. When you choose to think and feel the right things, you take control of your story, you write a different ending, and you define your life.

Your thinking story is defined by your subconscious beliefs, patterns, pictures, and stories. As the writer of this story, you can change it. It exists in your mind, and with some shifts of your thinking, you can change it.

The statement: "I cannot" does not exist in reality. It only has a place in your thoughts and emotions, and you can change your mind about it. Do not repeat this kind of thinking. You can change it. You can move past it, and you can coach yourself to think something that is more empowering. You can accept and you can look for the right meaning. You can

choose to feel the way you choose to

feel. You can choose to think and feel the

way that is best for you.

When you change your mindset, you not

only change your life, but you change

your reality. It is all in your mind. You

can change your life story and let it

move you positively.

The mind is a powerful thing. It drives

your reality. It can be a powerful friend

or a formidable foe, depending on the

thoughts you choose to follow. It will

help you to thrive if you allow it to. It will keep you stuck if you let it get in the way.

As the main character in your story, you have the power to tell your own story, to write your own destiny. You are the master of your mind. You can choose to create whatever you want. You control your thoughts and your emotions. You ARE in control of your life.

Logic and Analytical Thinking

Now we addressed the question: what are methodological competencies? Now, we may wonder, how do you profit from System Thinking skills?

Enhancing your System Thinking skills isn't a small feat; it has several benefits to become a more effective problem solver: analytical abilities make you marketable: this is one of the most measurable and practical benefits of enhancing your analytics and System Thinking skills.

With the improvement of each of the above analytical skills, you would be more marketable, hirable at once.

Now, if you have your dream work already, fantastic! Learning these skills will help you shine in your employer's eyes and allow you to work better in less time.

Nonetheless, learning how to develop System Thinking skills will help you achieve this role you were looking for if you don't have your dream job.

Glide into your CV a few analytical skills, and your future boss will be very impressed.

Analytical skills help you solve the problem better: an effective imaginative problem solver lets you quickly tackle even the most daunting cognitive issues. In reality, when you know how data can be digested, the relevant information extracted, and a creative solution created, nothing can stand in the way and what you want.

Practical problem-solving at home, at work, or for a personal project would motivate you to succeed tomorrow.

Strategic thinking is encouraged through analytical skills: What is System Thinking? It is a type of intellectual discipline that emphasizes rational knowledge synthesis to generate informed thought and action.

It means we can interact with knowledge, experience, and even other people without reacting so often. The more conscious, the less reactive, we love, we love. And as we begin to think objectively, we pave the way for stronger interpersonal relationships.

In this stage of the problem-solving dilemma, the brain gathers the information that will later give us the tools to create a resolution to the problem at hand. It is always seeking information. The information coming into the brain starts to be organized and shuffled to make sense of what the outside world is doing. At this stage, mostly what is happing is just getting the information, assessing the situation, and looking for an answer to the problem.

Analytical thinking uses the sense to gather information. A person has been transported to a hospital after a severe car accident. The emergency room nurse will evaluate the person and ask questions to gather information to improve the patient's health and current situation. Watching vitals and how the patient is responding to different evaluations will determine how the nurse will take the steps needed to save this patient's life. Analytical thinking gathers the information in the world so the brain can determine the solution to the current problem.

A great way to create a more vital analytical thinking skill is to practice. The walkout in the world and just observe the surroundings. Be mindful of what is going on, look at details, and notice your interest.

Create questions about how things work and understand the concept. Games are another great way to improve the analytical mind. Research online and find brain games that will help you improve your brain function. When resolving a problem, look at the pros and cons of the issue. Be intentional in your decision making and recognize the consequences of your decision.

How to Develop Analytical Thinking Skills in 5 Easy Steps

Would it not apply to become a more strategic thinker with more robust analytical skills? Working to improve and develop your analytical skills will certainly not hurt!

Below are a few steps to begin developing more vital analytical skills: Play brain games: It is a fun and realistic way to get started to improve your analytical abilities and increase your brain capacity. So 15 minutes a day is what you need!

An ideal way to continue improving your System Thinking skills is to download a brain training app to test your cognitive skills.

You can access several approved applications to develop your analytical skills:

- Luminosity
- Elevate
- Eidetic

- Wizard

- Happily

- Brain Wave

Each day, learn something new: make it your habit to learn something new every day.

Most of us, once completed with education, are much more passive in our research.

We read when we need to, we learn new skills, but we never try emotional and cognitive stimulation entirely by ourselves.

Ok, strive to know something that excites your passions every day. Go online and look for a topic that has always fascinated you. Speak to an expert in a field in which you are interested. Go out and broaden your knowledge base the day before by knowing something you didn't know.

Therefore, not only can you read more by entering the book club, but you can also participate in direct review and discussion at book club meetings.

You have the opportunity to discuss the theoretical study, analyze metaphors and unpack symbolism.

And you can even make some friends in the process!

Volunteering in new projects: If you are interested in a particular analytical ability, why not volunteer for a project involving this ability?

Sometimes, we need a little inner drive to get into something different. We can't wait for anything in our lap yet. We must

to be able to go out there and do it
ourselves every once and a while.

If you want to learn new analytical skills
to apply to your arsenal, volunteer for
projects and activities to bring you
through the training first!

Take an online course: first, you will
determine what appeals to you the most
if you want to develop your analytical
skills.

Endure in mind that you may already
have some of the above analytical skills.

Everyone has different strengths and
weaknesses, so it is essential to decide
where you lie.

Why? And if we follow what we already
know, we only can't discover something
new — or do any favors for ourselves.

If you want to develop your analytical
arsenal, you have to try something you
haven't learned yet.

Perhaps you would like to develop your
research skills. Perhaps you may like to
try your hand in data processing and
reporting.

If you like, do some work to see what can be found online.

You will take an in-person course nearby. And you may sign up to obtain distance education from your home comfort.

You will take a constructive approach to develop your analytical skills. So, decide for yourself what you want, and go for it!

Your passion for success is the secret to growing your System Thinking skills and developing your analytical skills.

You can prepare yourself for tomorrow's triumphs, but only if you find the door to go through can you take the appropriate steps to open it.

Each of us can do unique and beautiful things.

So, what would you like to do with your future? The person you want to be is all about focused, deliberate action.

Think about where you want to change the most. Define your weaknesses, define your strengths. Find your

strengths, find your weaknesses.

And become more vital than you ever

dreamed of before.

Creative Thinking

Creativity is not solely about being an artist. Product managers need to be creative just as much as musicians, ballet dancers, or sculptors. Creative thinking is a crucial skill for all product managers to succeed in today's dynamic, complex, and interdependent global business environment (Gundry et al., 2016).

Creating new products, developing countermeasures to problems, planning research projects, improving processes, and creating product education workshops require creative thinking skills. Generating and implementing new ideas is critical to the organization's success or failure (Bergendahl & Magnussion, 2015). Due to today's business environment's complexity and volatility, it is critical to continually develop new ideas (Sinfield et al., 2014).

Most people greatly underuse creativity based on society's conditioning

processes, educational systems, and
business organizations (Nolan, 1989).

Most adults feel they are not creative;
however, their creative abilities have just
atrophied – they are not lost. Learning
creative thinking tools and techniques,
practicing, and creating an environment
where critical judgment is suspended,
and speculation encouraged to form the
foundation for creating innovative
products, services, and processes.

You need to become skilled at
developing new ideas and any place,

then putting those ideas into practice to develop innovative solutions. Search for new possibilities and actively use the information around you (de Bono, 1992). Explore new ways of thinking and challenge firmly held assumptions (Zaltman et al., 1982). Most importantly, discover and exploit opportunities to create competitive advantages and innovative solutions; do not wait for opportunities to appear (Gundry et al., 2016).

Creative thinking aims to develop new and better ways to do things (de Bono, 1992).

When developing new ideas, focus on "what could be" and "what if" rather than "what is." Challenge tradition and current concepts and not be afraid of being wrong (de Bono, 1992).

Ignore "killer phrases," which stifle creativity; for example, "It won't work," "We tried that before," or "It's not practical" (Biech, 1996). Do not allow the status quo to handcuff you and suppress creativity (Brandt & Eagleman,

2017). Not innovating is the most significant risk to poor performance (never doing anything new or never seeking alternatives) (Nolan, 1989).

Move beyond necessary business housekeeping activities (e.g., cutting costs, improving quality, enhancing customer service) and develop new ideas to drive future growth (de Bono, 1992).

Focus on areas with no apparent problems and identify ways to improve these "perfect" areas (de Bono, 1992). Break things that are working fine. Focus on areas that you are not interested in or that because you discomfort; face challenges head-on and continually improve (Trott, 2015).

Create new ideas individually and then develop the ideas collectively with a cross-functional team (Carucci, 2017).

Research has shown individual ideation to result in a higher quantity of quality, practical, and useable ideas than group ideation (Schirr, 2012).

The goal of creative thinking is to create many ideas (divergent thinking). It is not about judging ideas: you do that during critical thinking (convergent thinking).

Do not try to develop new ideas ad hoc, or you will be wasting time – the most effective way to develop new ideas is with a deliberate, structured, and systematic process.

Using a systematic process for creativity may sound counterintuitive; however, research has shown that participants developed a higher number of ideas when using a systematic process than ad hoc methods (Schirr, 2012).

James Webb Young (1960) identified a five-step creative process to develop new ideas.

1. Gather materials

2. Digest the information

3. Ignore the information – let it incubate (e.g., go for a walk, go to a movie)

4. An idea will appear out of nowhere

5. Apply the idea to the real world

Graham Wallas (2014) identified a similar process.

1. Preparation

2. Incubation

3. Illumination

4. Verification

Young and Wallas both noted that new ideas are typically combinations of many unrelated items. Developing creative ideas requires you to "connect the dots" from many different sources and experiences, aligning and combining unrelated areas.

As your ideas incubate in your unconscious mind, the ideas expand and elaborate until a creative breakthrough emerges (Morris, 1992).

Most "new ideas" are the reconstruction of things you already know or have experienced.

For example, smartphones combine the telephone, camera, internet, and voice recorder into a straightforward device. The snowmobile is a combination of a tractor, motorcycle, and snow skis. Continually exploring various subjects and exposing yourself to new experiences is critical to connecting unrelated "dots" to create new innovative ideas.

Connecting disparate areas of study provides an endless supply of ingredients for new ideas. When you ask questions, experience new things, and develop a thorough understanding of the topic, you will create new ideas and develop innovative solutions to develop new opportunities.

The challenge of creative thinking is balancing structure and flexibility, divergent and convergent thinking, individual and group ideation, productivity and creativity, and art and science (Carucci, 2017).

It is about overcoming mental blocks such as there is only one right answer, the idea is not logical, or you have to follow the rules (Jorgenson, 2018).

You must work hard to overcome society's rigid, rule-driven, constraining systems (Ackoff & Rovin, 2005).

Creative thinking is exploring new ideas and exploiting existing ideas.

It is difficult to get people out of their comfort zones and to move beyond the status quo (old habits die hard); however, for continued growth, you must become comfortable developing new ideas and challenging long-held beliefs – you must become comfortable with being uncomfortable.

Adapt to change and reimagine the world (Brandt & Eagleman, 2007).

Most importantly, do not overanalyze or judge your new ideas. Also, do not dismiss or abandon a new idea until you have given it sufficient time to develop.

Definitions

Four critical terms in creative thinking are imagination, creativity, innovation, and invention.

Creativity is developing new ideas: coming up with something new and original (Jorgenson, 2018).

It is applied imagination: taking your wild thoughts and developing new ideas (Robinson, 2017). It is a continuous process of discovering and solving problems.

Creativity is the capacity to find new and unexpected connections and find new relationships: a mindset that anything is possible (Prince, 2012).

Mindlessly following rules does not lead to creativity. Creativity is about challenging or denying assumptions that constrain you from achieving what you want to accomplish (Ackoff & Rovin, 2005).

Good ideas are a dime a dozen. It is only after a new idea is translated into a reality that it becomes valuable: an innovation (Nolan, 1989).

Innovation is the procedure of implementing creative ideas and introducing something new (Robinson, 2017).

It is figuring out how to take a new idea and turn it into a product or service (Jorgenson, 2018).

The invention is creating something new that has never been developed. Merriam-Webster's online dictionary (2019) defines an invention as "to produce (something, such as a useful device or process) for the first time through the use of the imaginings or ingenious thinking and experiment."

New and improved ideas are the foundation for future success. Building the skills to develop new ideas any time and any place is critical for developing new products, devising effective marketing campaigns, or planning new product launches to confuse and surprise your competitors.

An organization focused on continuous improvement will continuously be on the lookout for opportunities where new ideas can transform the business.

Society

People are creative, constructive, and exploratory beings, so why does creativity seem so difficult (Norman, 2013)? Why don't more people develop great new ideas?

Unfortunately, creativity is often discouraged by our educational systems and business organizations.

Also, society values adult practicality, consistency, and rigidity, diminishing our creative abilities and the desire to look beyond the obvious for alternative answers (Prince, 2012).

Society values logic and judgment over imagination. As we mature, we undergo a conditioning process that suppresses our creativity (Basadur, 1995).

Childhood playfulness is discouraged as we grow older and become engaged with traditional society.

Most of our creative skills atrophy due to societal influences, attitudes, behaviors, and thought processes (Basadur, 1995).

The educational system is the leading cause of the lack of creativity in adults and organizations. Informal education, we learn what's acceptable and what's not (von Oech, 1998).

Teachers typically have an expected, acceptable answer for questions or problems (Ackoff & Rovin, 2005).

We are taught how to solve problems rather than look for opportunities. Throughout our schooling, we are taught to find the right answer, not to look for alternatives. Children are continually taught limitations instead of searching for many different options (Prince, 2012).

It is essential to challenge the establishment and "color outside the lines continually."

The educational system also awards students for following the rules, rather than developing many new ideas and thinking originally (von Oech, 1998).

Rules and the insistence on conformity puts a chokehold on children's innate, natural curiosity (Ackoff & Rovin, 2005).

As adults, we too often accept workplace norms without question.

Yes, it is essential to follow a variety of rules to survive in society (e.g., do not scream "fire" in a public place, stop at a red traffic light, raise your hand when wanting to speak); however, if you never challenge the rules or discard your "sacred cows" you will never be able to see the benefits of alternative ideas (von Oech, 1998).

There are benefits to conforming to societal norms, for example, cooperating with others and learning by observing how others react (von Oech, 1998).

However, you need to challenge the status quo and live with a revolutionary mindset to create innovative products and services. You need courage, confidence, and persistence to achieve your dreams (Ackoff & Rovin, 2005).

Another reason for lack of creativity is that most people haven't been taught how to develop new ideas. Most people use ad hoc methods when new ideas are needed.

However, creative thinking is a skill, and like other skills such as ice skating, cooking, or singing, it is developed by learning the basics and then practicing.

Unfortunately, the majority of schools never teach structured methods for ideation. Most people struggle through life, trying to "think up" new ideas.

Finally, your own beliefs may prevent you from seeking new ideas (von Oech, 1998).

Your schooling, religion, and community influence how you think and perceive the world.

These "mental blocks" prevent you from proactively changing routine or moving beyond what is familiar (von Oech, 1998). Creativity is a skill and mindset.

Learn the tools and techniques and adopt a mindset that strives for seeking multiple perspectives and a large number of possible alternatives.

Know Yourself

**manage your thoughts,
uses analytical thinking and creative
thinking**

Ray Crystal

Know Yourself through

Thought patterns

Remove Negative Influences Cut Off

Destroying Thoughts

Negative energy is everywhere. You can

find it at every turn. Negative energy can

take the form of unhappy people, violent content on television, or even environmental damage. You can see this consistently. No matter where you go, you will encounter charges of negative energy.

And while there isn't much, you can do to stop negative energy from swirling around in the world, and there is plenty that you can do to stop it from taking over your mind. When you find yourself immersed in a hostile environment, it is straightforward to get caught up in the situation's negativity.

For instance, you are working in a very hostile environment. Your boss and co-workers aren't getting along, which leads to an overall unpleasant atmosphere. At this point, you have one of two choices, you either let that get to you, or you don't. Of course, it's not quite that simple.

One of the most effective ways to avoid being brought down by this type of atmosphere is to stop it from getting to you merely. You can learn to recognize the onset of negative thoughts and emotions. When you do, you can nip them in the bud. You can make use of mantras such as "negative energies can't touch me" or "negative thoughts are like a ship passing in the night."

In other words, don't let negative thoughts pull up a chair and have a seat. If you allow them to do that, you are opening the door to trouble. The main thing to keep in mind is that you are the master of your thoughts and emotions. The only way something can get to you is if you let it.

However, indeed, a highly hostile environment will undoubtedly charge you with negative energy. In that case, it is always a great idea to have ways in which you can unload those energies. That is why pleasant activities are needed at the end of the day. That way, you can simply let go of the energies which are negatively affecting you.

Secrets to Successfully Tame Your Thoughts

If people knew that succeeding in life depended on their actions, they would be less likely to worry about their lives. At times, we go through life with regrets and anxiety. We don't feel ready to let go of the feelings that we have embedded within us. Concerning our future, we worry about tomorrow, but a large number of people don't know the power that they have. The power that you have within you can quickly become a destructive force or a constructive force that will push you to succeed in life. You have the power to control your life and live it as you wish. What you think about is what you become. If you keep thinking that you will always struggle in life, rest assured that you will struggle to keep things afloat. Conversely, if you genuinely believe that everything will fall into place and that your time will come for you to enjoy life, expect to live a life full of optimism.

Listen to Yourself

To tame your thoughts, start by listening to yourself. Do this as though you were explaining something to other people. How would you want to tell other people about the story of your life? Without a doubt, you would want to talk about everything that you have done well. No one would want to tell others negative stories about themselves. Therefore, you should adopt a similar attitude when listening to yourself. Focus on treating yourself with the same respect that you would expect from other people. This means that you should strive to focus on thoughts that put you in a positive light.

Your Inner Self is Listening

Besides, you should always bear in mind that your inner self is listening to your thoughts; this is the inner you. So, if you continue thinking about negative things, your inner self will listen and conform to how you expect it to behave. When thinking positively, it will also listen to you and adapt to help you perceive life with optimism. Therefore, before blaming other people for the bad things

that are happening to you, remember that
there is someone within you who is
listening to your self-talk.

Befriend Your Emotional Guidance System

The point here is that you should pause
every time you notice that your emotions
have changed. You should take some
time to evaluate your emotions and the
next thoughts before they gain
momentum. The effect of this is that it
will help you develop an attitude of
thinking twice before doing anything.

Before doing anything, you will reflect on whether what you're about to do is favorable or not. You increase the likelihood of making the right decisions without allowing emotions to cloud your judgment.

Find Your Stop Signs

Another practical tip that can make a difference in how you think is visualizing stop signs that signal to you that you should stop thinking about something. Your stop signs will warrant that you regain your senses and avoid thinking about your past or worrying about your future. The best way of using these stop signs is to remind you that your thoughts are not helping to build you up. For instance, you can come up with a stop sign that reminds you that you are overthinking about events that prevent you from being happy. It might take some time for you to master how to use these stop signs, but the outcome will be rewarding as it will enhance your self-awareness.

Consider Words as Your Nutrition

When thinking about improving our health, we know perfectly that eating right can only be done. The foods that you choose to eat have an impact on your health. In the same manner, the words that float around in your mind impact your mental health. This means that it is essential that you control the information that you feed into your mind. For example, watching horrific content on television might not be as entertaining as you think. In the long run, this will harm how you think and the thoughts that frequent your mind.

Remind Yourself with Affirmations

Becoming the master of your mind also demands that you stay on top of your game. You have to keep yourself engaged in festive gear. Sure, there are instances when you might slip up and think negatively, but with the right affirmations, you will feel unstoppable. Have these affirmations in areas where you can easily see them. Pin them next to your files in your office. Before going to bed, remind yourself of your higher purpose by reading out these affirmations to yourself. They can eliminate anxiety and soothe you to sleep better.

Take Out the Trash

Increasing your self-awareness about your thoughts will give you the advantage of identifying unnecessary thoughts and emotions. When you do this steadily, you will find it easier to declutter your mind. The notion of taking out the trash shouldn't drive you to overthink about your past. Instead, the point here is to develop an attitude where you simply admit that some thoughts are not worth holding on to. Practice meditation exercises as a method of increasing your self-awareness. This is the best way of raising your antennas high enough to pick any signals of unwanted thoughts in your mind.

Pursue Meaning Over Pleasure

There is a good reason why you should strive to be happy. Most people have never realized that there are adverse effects of focusing too much on striving for positivity. Sure, we all want our lives to be full of happiness. However, we should come to terms with the fact that too much of anything is detrimental. This also applies to happiness. When we go about chasing happiness, we surround ourselves with all the things that can keep us entertained and full of joy. The downside of this kind of life is that it can blind us to unrealistic optimism.

Flex Your Muscle Memory

Technology has changed the way we access information in today's world. The digital devices that we have been introduced to make it easy for us to consume information than ever before. However, this affects our muscle memory since we rely too much on these devices. You can find Millennials struggling with simple calculations where they have to turn to their smartphones. According to a study, to some extent, seniors from the Baby Boomer generation have better memory compared to Millennials.

Take Control Over Your Thought Patterns

A "controlled thinking" mindset helps you to shift your focus intentionally. It allows you to determine your performance, rather than getting stuck replaying negative experiences in your head. You have to purposefully choose to focus on what you want instead.

In order to choose where you want to put your attention, you need to take control of your mind, thoughts, and emotions.

You are only as stuck or as free as your

mindset allows you to be. It is the story

of good or bad experiences your mind

tells you. It is the story of your life. It is

the imprint of your mind.

The mind is an incredible machine.

When given the right kind of input, it can

produce amazing results. It is a habitual

learner. It wants to adapt to its

environment, including whatever

patterns of thoughts, emotions, and

actions you expose it to. It can also adapt

to change. As its owner, you have the

power to rewrite the story. You can choose to override the negative, limiting thoughts and emotions. You can decide to tell a different story and one that will empower you. You must intentionally choose to change your thinking and take control of your life.

To shift your mindset, you must first identify your habitual thoughts and emotions and then learn to shift them intentionally (not simply by willpower) by creating a better story.

You take control of where you focus your attention. You can choose to think or you can choose to feel. When you choose to think and feel the right things, you take control of your story, you write a different ending, and you define your life.

The key to transformation lies in you. It all starts with the story your mind tells you. Your mind is defined by your thoughts and emotions. You are a habitual thinker. You do not typically think of something once and decide to never think about it again. Your thoughts initiative your emotions which in turn shape your responses and behaviors. Because your mind is a "habitual" learner, it will automatically and repetitively go to the place where you decide to take it.

You take control of where you focus your attention. You can choose to think or you can choose to feel. When you choose to think and feel the right things, you take control of your story, you write a different ending, and you define your life.

Your thinking story is defined by your subconscious beliefs, patterns, pictures, and stories. As the writer of this story, you can change it. It exists in your mind, and with some shifts of your thinking, you can change it.

The statement: "I cannot" does not exist in reality. It only has a place in your thoughts and emotions, and you can change your mind about it. Do not repeat this kind of thinking. You can change it. You can move past it, and you can coach yourself to think something that is more empowering. You can accept and you can look for the right meaning. You can choose to feel the way you choose to feel. You can choose to think and feel the way that is best for you.

When you change your mindset, you not only change your life, but you change your reality. It is all in your mind. You can change your life story and let it move you positively.

The mind is a powerful thing. It drives your reality. It can be a powerful friend or a formidable foe, depending on the thoughts you choose to follow. It will help you to thrive if you allow it to. It will keep you stuck if you let it get in the way.

As the main character in your story, you have the power to tell your own story, to write your own destiny. You are the master of your mind. You can choose to create whatever you want. You control your thoughts and your emotions. You ARE in control of your life.

Logic and Analytical Thinking

Now we addressed the question: what are methodological competencies? Now, we may wonder, how do you profit from System Thinking skills?

Enhancing your System Thinking skills isn't a small feat; it has several benefits to become a more effective problem solver: analytical abilities make you marketable: this is one of the most measurable and practical benefits of enhancing your analytics and System Thinking skills.

With the improvement of each of the above analytical skills, you would be more marketable, hirable at once.

Now, if you have your dream work already, fantastic! Learning these skills will help you shine in your employer's eyes and allow you to work better in less time.

Nonetheless, learning how to develop System Thinking skills will help you achieve this role you were looking for if you don't have your dream job.

Glide into your CV a few analytical skills, and your future boss will be very impressed.

Analytical skills help you solve the problem better: an effective imaginative problem solver lets you quickly tackle even the most daunting cognitive issues. In reality, when you know how data can be digested, the relevant information extracted, and a creative solution created, nothing can stand in the way and what you want.

Practical problem-solving at home, at work, or for a personal project would motivate you to succeed tomorrow.

Strategic thinking is encouraged through analytical skills: What is System Thinking? It is a type of intellectual discipline that emphasizes rational knowledge synthesis to generate informed thought and action.

It means we can interact with knowledge, experience, and even other people without reacting so often. The more conscious, the less reactive, we love, we love. And as we begin to think objectively, we pave the way for stronger interpersonal relationships.

In this stage of the problem-solving dilemma, the brain gathers the information that will later give us the tools to create a resolution to the problem at hand. It is always seeking information. The information coming into the brain starts to be organized and shuffled to make sense of what the outside world is doing. At this stage, mostly what is happing is just getting the information, assessing the situation, and looking for an answer to the problem.

Analytical thinking uses the sense to gather information. A person has been transported to a hospital after a severe car accident. The emergency room nurse will evaluate the person and ask questions to gather information to improve the patient's health and current situation. Watching vitals and how the patient is responding to different evaluations will determine how the nurse will take the steps needed to save this patient's life. Analytical thinking gathers the information in the world so the brain can determine the solution to the current problem.

A great way to create a more vital analytical thinking skill is to practice. The walkout in the world and just observe the surroundings. Be mindful of what is going on, look at details, and notice your interest.

Create questions about how things work and understand the concept. Games are another great way to improve the analytical mind. Research online and find brain games that will help you improve your brain function. When resolving a problem, look at the pros and cons of the issue. Be intentional in your decision making and recognize the consequences of your decision.

How to Develop Analytical Thinking Skills in 5 Easy Steps

Would it not apply to become a more strategic thinker with more robust analytical skills? Working to improve and develop your analytical skills will certainly not hurt!

Below are a few steps to begin developing more vital analytical skills: Play brain games: It is a fun and realistic way to get started to improve your analytical abilities and increase your brain capacity. So 15 minutes a day is what you need!

An ideal way to continue improving your System Thinking skills is to download a brain training app to test your cognitive skills.

You can access several approved applications to develop your analytical skills:

- Luminosity
- Elevate
- Eidetic

- Wizard

- Happily

- Brain Wave

Each day, learn something new: make it your habit to learn something new every day.

Most of us, once completed with education, are much more passive in our research.

We read when we need to, we learn new skills, but we never try emotional and cognitive stimulation entirely by ourselves.

Ok, strive to know something that excites your passions every day. Go online and look for a topic that has always fascinated you. Speak to an expert in a field in which you are interested. Go out and broaden your knowledge base the day before by knowing something you didn't know.

Therefore, not only can you read more by entering the book club, but you can also participate in direct review and discussion at book club meetings.

You have the opportunity to discuss the theoretical study, analyze metaphors and unpack symbolism.

And you can even make some friends in the process!

Volunteering in new projects: If you are interested in a particular analytical ability, why not volunteer for a project involving this ability?

Sometimes, we need a little inner drive to get into something different. We can't wait for anything in our lap yet. We must to be able to go out there and do it ourselves every once and a while.

If you want to learn new analytical skills to apply to your arsenal, volunteer for projects and activities to bring you through the training first!

Take an online course: first, you will determine what appeals to you the most if you want to develop your analytical skills.

Endure in mind that you may already have some of the above analytical skills.

Everyone has different strengths and weaknesses, so it is essential to decide where you lie.

Why? And if we follow what we already know, we only can't discover something new — or do any favors for ourselves.

If you want to develop your analytical arsenal, you have to try something you haven't learned yet.

Perhaps you would like to develop your research skills. Perhaps you may like to try your hand in data processing and reporting.

If you like, do some work to see what
can be found online.

You will take an in-person course nearby.
And you may sign up to obtain distance
education from your home comfort.

You will take a constructive approach to
develop your analytical skills. So, decide
for yourself what you want, and go for it!

Your passion for success is the secret to
growing your System Thinking skills and
developing your analytical skills.

You can prepare yourself for tomorrow's triumphs, but only if you find the door to go through can you take the appropriate steps to open it.

Each of us can do unique and beautiful things.

So, what would you like to do with your future? The person you want to be is all about focused, deliberate action.

Think about where you want to change the most. Define your weaknesses, define your strengths. Find your

strengths, find your weaknesses.

And become more vital than you ever

dreamed of before.

Creative Thinking

Creativity is not solely about being an artist. Product managers need to be creative just as much as musicians, ballet dancers, or sculptors. Creative thinking is a crucial skill for all product managers to succeed in today's dynamic, complex, and interdependent global business environment (Gundry et al., 2016).

Creating new products, developing countermeasures to problems, planning research projects, improving processes, and creating product education workshops require creative thinking skills. Generating and implementing new ideas is critical to the organization's success or failure (Bergendahl & Magnussion, 2015). Due to today's business environment's complexity and volatility, it is critical to continually develop new ideas (Sinfield et al., 2014).

Most people greatly underuse creativity based on society's conditioning processes, educational systems, and business organizations (Nolan, 1989).

Most adults feel they are not creative; however, their creative abilities have just atrophied – they are not lost. Learning creative thinking tools and techniques, practicing, and creating an environment where critical judgment is suspended, and speculation encouraged to form the foundation for creating innovative products, services, and processes.

You need to become skilled at developing new ideas and any place, then putting those ideas into practice to develop innovative solutions. Search for new possibilities and actively use the information around you (de Bono, 1992). Explore new ways of thinking and challenge firmly held assumptions (Zaltman et al., 1982). Most importantly, discover and exploit opportunities to create competitive advantages and innovative solutions; do not wait for opportunities to appear (Gundry et al., 2016).

Creative thinking aims to develop new and better ways to do things (de Bono, 1992).

When developing new ideas, focus on "what could be" and "what if" rather than "what is." Challenge tradition and current concepts and not be afraid of being wrong (de Bono, 1992).

Ignore "killer phrases," which stifle creativity; for example, "It won't work," "We tried that before," or "It's not practical" (Biech, 1996). Do not allow the status quo to handcuff you and suppress creativity (Brandt & Eagleman,

2017). Not innovating is the most significant risk to poor performance (never doing anything new or never seeking alternatives) (Nolan, 1989).

Move beyond necessary business housekeeping activities (e.g., cutting costs, improving quality, enhancing customer service) and develop new ideas to drive future growth (de Bono, 1992).

Focus on areas with no apparent problems and identify ways to improve these "perfect" areas (de Bono, 1992). Break things that are working fine. Focus on areas that you are not interested in or that because you discomfort; face challenges head-on and continually improve (Trott, 2015).

Create new ideas individually and then develop the ideas collectively with a cross-functional team (Carucci, 2017).

Research has shown individual ideation to result in a higher quantity of quality, practical, and useable ideas than group ideation (Schirr, 2012).

The goal of creative thinking is to create many ideas (divergent thinking). It is not about judging ideas: you do that during critical thinking (convergent thinking).

Do not try to develop new ideas ad hoc, or you will be wasting time – the most effective way to develop new ideas is with a deliberate, structured, and systematic process.

Using a systematic process for creativity may sound counterintuitive; however, research has shown that participants developed a higher number of ideas when using a systematic process than ad hoc methods (Schirr, 2012).

James Webb Young (1960) identified a five-step creative process to develop new ideas.

1. Gather materials

2. Digest the information

3. Ignore the information – let it incubate (e.g., go for a walk, go to a movie)

4. An idea will appear out of nowhere

5. Apply the idea to the real world

Graham Wallas (2014) identified a similar process.

1. Preparation

2. Incubation

3. Illumination

4. Verification

Young and Wallas both noted that new ideas are typically combinations of many unrelated items. Developing creative ideas requires you to "connect the dots" from many different sources and experiences, aligning and combining unrelated areas.

As your ideas incubate in your unconscious mind, the ideas expand and elaborate until a creative breakthrough emerges (Morris, 1992).

Most "new ideas" are the reconstruction of things you already know or have experienced.

For example, smartphones combine the telephone, camera, internet, and voice recorder into a straightforward device. The snowmobile is a combination of a tractor, motorcycle, and snow skis. Continually exploring various subjects and exposing yourself to new experiences is critical to connecting unrelated "dots" to create new innovative ideas.

Connecting disparate areas of study provides an endless supply of ingredients for new ideas. When you ask questions, experience new things, and develop a thorough understanding of the topic, you will create new ideas and develop innovative solutions to develop new opportunities.

The challenge of creative thinking is balancing structure and flexibility, divergent and convergent thinking, individual and group ideation, productivity and creativity, and art and science (Carucci, 2017).

It is about overcoming mental blocks such as there is only one right answer, the idea is not logical, or you have to follow the rules (Jorgenson, 2018).

You must work hard to overcome society's rigid, rule-driven, constraining systems (Ackoff & Rovin, 2005).

Creative thinking is exploring new ideas and exploiting existing ideas.

It is difficult to get people out of their comfort zones and to move beyond the status quo (old habits die hard); however, for continued growth, you must become comfortable developing new ideas and challenging long-held beliefs – you must become comfortable with being uncomfortable.

Adapt to change and reimagine the world (Brandt & Eagleman, 2007).

Most importantly, do not overanalyze or judge your new ideas. Also, do not dismiss or abandon a new idea until you have given it sufficient time to develop.

Definitions

Four critical terms in creative thinking are imagination, creativity, innovation, and invention.

Creativity is developing new ideas: coming up with something new and original (Jorgenson, 2018).

It is applied imagination: taking your wild thoughts and developing new ideas (Robinson, 2017). It is a continuous process of discovering and solving problems.

Creativity is the capacity to find new and unexpected connections and find new relationships: a mindset that anything is possible (Prince, 2012).

Mindlessly following rules does not lead to creativity. Creativity is about challenging or denying assumptions that constrain you from achieving what you want to accomplish (Ackoff & Rovin, 2005).

Good ideas are a dime a dozen. It is only after a new idea is translated into a reality that it becomes valuable: an innovation (Nolan, 1989).

Innovation is the procedure of implementing creative ideas and introducing something new (Robinson, 2017).

It is figuring out how to take a new idea and turn it into a product or service (Jorgenson, 2018).

The invention is creating something new that has never been developed. Merriam-Webster's online dictionary (2019) defines an invention as "to produce (something, such as a useful device or process) for the first time through the use of the imaginings or ingenious thinking and experiment."

New and improved ideas are the foundation for future success. Building the skills to develop new ideas any time and any place is critical for developing new products, devising effective marketing campaigns, or planning new product launches to confuse and surprise your competitors.

An organization focused on continuous improvement will continuously be on the lookout for opportunities where new ideas can transform the business.

Society

People are creative, constructive, and exploratory beings, so why does creativity seem so difficult (Norman, 2013)? Why don't more people develop great new ideas?

Unfortunately, creativity is often discouraged by our educational systems and business organizations.

Also, society values adult practicality, consistency, and rigidity, diminishing our creative abilities and the desire to look beyond the obvious for alternative answers (Prince, 2012).

Society values logic and judgment over imagination. As we mature, we undergo a conditioning process that suppresses our creativity (Basadur, 1995).

Childhood playfulness is discouraged as we grow older and become engaged with traditional society.

Most of our creative skills atrophy due to societal influences, attitudes, behaviors, and thought processes (Basadur, 1995).

The educational system is the leading cause of the lack of creativity in adults and organizations. Informal education, we learn what's acceptable and what's not (von Oech, 1998).

Teachers typically have an expected, acceptable answer for questions or problems (Ackoff & Rovin, 2005).

We are taught how to solve problems rather than look for opportunities. Throughout our schooling, we are taught to find the right answer, not to look for alternatives. Children are continually taught limitations instead of searching for many different options (Prince, 2012).

It is essential to challenge the establishment and "color outside the lines continually."

The educational system also awards students for following the rules, rather than developing many new ideas and thinking originally (von Oech, 1998).

Rules and the insistence on conformity puts a chokehold on children's innate, natural curiosity (Ackoff & Rovin, 2005).

As adults, we too often accept workplace norms without question.

Yes, it is essential to follow a variety of rules to survive in society (e.g., do not scream "fire" in a public place, stop at a red traffic light, raise your hand when wanting to speak); however, if you never challenge the rules or discard your "sacred cows" you will never be able to see the benefits of alternative ideas (von Oech, 1998).

There are benefits to conforming to societal norms, for example, cooperating with others and learning by observing how others react (von Oech, 1998).

However, you need to challenge the status quo and live with a revolutionary mindset to create innovative products and services. You need courage, confidence, and persistence to achieve your dreams (Ackoff & Rovin, 2005).

Another reason for lack of creativity is that most people haven't been taught how to develop new ideas. Most people use ad hoc methods when new ideas are needed.

However, creative thinking is a skill, and like other skills such as ice skating, cooking, or singing, it is developed by learning the basics and then practicing.

Unfortunately, the majority of schools never teach structured methods for ideation. Most people struggle through life, trying to "think up" new ideas.

Finally, your own beliefs may prevent you from seeking new ideas (von Oech, 1998).

Your schooling, religion, and community influence how you think and perceive the world.

These "mental blocks" prevent you from proactively changing routine or moving beyond what is familiar (von Oech, 1998). Creativity is a skill and mindset.

Learn the tools and techniques and adopt a mindset that strives for seeking multiple perspectives and a large number of possible alternatives.

CPSIA information can be obtained
at www.ICGtesting.com
Printed in the USA
BVHW071538270321
603572BV00005B/853